This book is full of healthy recipes perfect for the whole family. You'll find breakfast, lunch, and dinner ideas that are sure to please everyone's taste buds. The recipes have been carefully crafted to ensure healthy ingredients are included for a nutritious meal every time. Whether you're looking for something quick and easy or an elaborate dish suitable for a special occasion, you'll find something delicious in this book. All recipes have detailed instructions and nutritional information so you can make healthy choices with confidence. With the variety of recipes included, everyone in your family is sure to find something they love. Start cooking healthy meals for the whole family today!

Cheesy Broccoli Pasta

Ingredients
½ cup butter.
1 onion, chopped. Fresh Onions.
1 (16 ounce) package frozen chopped broccoli.
4 (14.5 ounce) cans chicken broth.
1 (1 pound) loaf processed cheese food, cubed.
2 cups milk.
1 tablespoon garlic powder.
⅔ cup cornstarch.

This delicious cheesy broccoli pasta is a sure hit for kids and adults alike! With just a few simple steps, anyone can make this delicious dish in no time.

First, melt the butter in a large pot over medium heat. Add the chopped onion and cook until softened, about 5 minutes. Next, add the frozen chopped broccoli and chicken broth and bring to a boil. Reduce the heat, cover, and simmer for 15 minutes.

Once done, add the cubed cheese food, milk, garlic powder and cornstarch to the pot. Give it all a good stir then cover and cook for about 10 more minutes or until the sauce has thickened. Serve hot with your favorite sides!

This cheesy broccoli pasta is delicious and easy to make, making it an ideal recipe for kids. If you're looking for a delicious and nutritious dish that your whole family can enjoy, this is the perfect choice! So what are you waiting for? Try out this delicious cheesy broccoli pasta today!

Enjoy

Tacos

Vegetarian tacos are a great way to introduce vegetarian recipes to kids. This vegetarian taco recipe is simple and delicious, using quick-pickled onions, creamy avocado dip, easy refried beans and 8 corn tortillas. To top it off, add some salsa verde, shredded green cabbage for extra crunch, fresh cilantro and lime wedges. These vegetarian tacos are healthy, tasty options that can easily be added to your family's meal rotation! Kids will love these vegetarian tacos - they're sure to become a favorite! Try this vegetarian taco recipe today and enjoy the yummy benefits of vegetarian cooking with your family!

To make vegetarian tacos, start by preparing the quick-pickled onions. Then, prepare the creamy avocado dip and easy refried beans. Warm up 8 corn tortillas in a pan over medium heat for about 15 seconds on each side. Fill each taco with a spoonful of refried beans and top them off with some salsa verde, shredded green cabbage, cilantro, and lime wedges. Enjoy vegetarian tacos - healthy recipes for kids that are sure to be a hit!

Vegetarian tacos are an easy way to incorporate vegetarian recipes into your family's meal rotation while still keeping everyone happy. With quick-pickled onions, creamy avocado dip, easy refried beans and warm corn tortillas, these vegetarian tacos are sure to be a hit with kids and adults alike. Enjoy vegetarian tacos for a healthy and delicious meal that your whole family will love!

Try this vegetarian taco recipe today and enjoy the yummy benefits of vegetarian cooking with your family! It's easy to make, healthy, and the perfect vegetarian recipes for kids. Start by preparing the quick-pickled onions, creamy avocado dip, and easy refried beans. Warm up 8 corn tortillas in a pan over medium heat for 15 seconds on each side. Toppings include salsa verde, shredded green cabbage, cilantro, and lime wedges. Serve vegetarian tacos as an easy way to get everyone excited about vegetarian meals!
Enjoy!

Spinach Alfredo Pizza

Ingredients

1 13 oz puff pastry sheet.
½ cup Alfredo sauce any jar or type will work.
12 oz. marinated artichoke hearts chopped.
1 cup fresh spinach leaves.
2 Tbsp. green onions chopped.
8 oz. log mozzarella cheese sliced.
½ cup parmesan cheese shredded.
1 Tbsp. Everything Bagel seasoning ad.!

This delicious Spinach Alfredo Pizza is a great way to enjoy a delicious pizza without having to order from your favorite pizzeria. With its delicious combination of Alfredo sauce, artichoke hearts, spinach, and mozzarella cheese, this pizza will be sure to satisfy even the pickiest of eaters.

To prepare this delicious pizza, start by preheating your oven to 375 degrees Fahrenheit. Then unroll the puff pastry sheet onto a greased baking sheet or round stone. Spread the Alfredo sauce over the entire sheet until evenly covered and sprinkle with chopped artichoke hearts, fresh spinach leaves and green onions. Top with sliced mozzarella cheese and shredded parmesan cheese before sprinkling with everything bagel seasoning.

Bake in your preheated oven for 25-30 minutes or until the cheese is golden and bubbly. Let cool slightly before serving and enjoy!

This delicious Spinach Alfredo Pizza is one of many delicious pizza recipes you can make at home and it's sure to be a hit with everyone in the family. Give this delicious pizza recipe a try today and let us know how it turns out! Enjoy!

Baked Feta Pasta

ingredients

2 pints (20 oz) grape tomatoes.
1/2 cup extra-virgin olive oil.
Salt and freshly ground black pepper.
7 oz. block feta cheese (sheep's milk variety), drained.
10 oz. dry pasta (bite size)
5 medium garlic cloves, peeled and halved.
8 oz. ...
1/4 tsp crushed red pepper flakes, or more to taste.

Baked Feta Pasta is an easy and healthy dish that takes only minimal time to prepare. With just a handful of simple ingredients, you can create this delicious meal. To make it, start by preheating your oven to 425 degrees Fahrenheit.

In a large bowl, combine the grape tomatoes, extra-virgin olive oil, salt and pepper. Cut the feta cheese into small cubes and add it to the bowl. Next, cook 10 oz of bite-size pasta according to package instructions until al dente. Once done, drain it and mix it with the tomato mixture in the bowl.

Add garlic cloves, 8 oz of mushrooms (sliced), and 1/4 tsp of crushed red pepper flakes, or to taste. Toss everything together and spread it in a single layer on an oven-safe dish. Bake for 25 minutes until the top is lightly golden brown.

Baked Feta Pasta is now ready to enjoy! Serve with a sprinkling of fresh herbs, extra olive oil, and a side of crusty bread. This healthy pasta dish makes for a great weeknight dinner that is sure to please the whole family. Enjoy!

Easy Pesto Pasta

INGREDIENTS

6 OUNCES SPAGHETTI, RESERVE 1/2 CUP STARCHY PASTA WATER.
1/3 TO 1/2 CUP. BASIL PESTO OR VEGAN PESTO.
EXTRA-VIRGIN OLIVE OIL, FOR DRIZZLING.
FRESH LEMON JUICE, AS DESIRED.
4 CUPS ARUGULA.
2 TABLESPOONS PINE NUTS.
PINCHES OF RED PEPPER FLAKES.
SEA SALT AND FRESHLY GROUND BLACK PEPPER.

This healthy pesto pasta dish is an easy way to put together a delicious meal in no time! To make it, start by cooking the spaghetti according to the instructions on the package. Once cooked, reserve 1/2 cup of starchy pasta water and set aside. In a large bowl, combine the basil pesto or vegan pesto with the arugula and pine nuts. Stir until everything is evenly combined, then add a splash of extra-virgin olive oil and fresh lemon juice as desired. Finally, pour in the starchy pasta water and season with red pepper flakes, sea salt, and freshly ground black pepper to taste. Serve hot! With its combination of healthy ingredients like arugula and pine nuts, this pesto pasta dish is sure to satisfy your appetite without sacrificing on flavor. Enjoy!

For a vegan-friendly version of this recipe, simply substitute the basil pesto with an equivalent amount of vegan pesto. You can also swap out the arugula for any other leafy green vegetables you have available. Feel free to experiment and make it your own! Bon appétit!

Fish And Chips

Ingredients

900 g potatoes.
sunflower oil , for deep-frying.
225 g white fish fillets , skin off, pin-boned, from sustainable sources.
225 g plain flour , plus extra for dusting.
285 ml cold beer.
3 heaped teaspoons baking powder.
MUSHY PEAS.
a few sprigs of fresh mint.

Fish and chips is a classic dish that's loved by many! With just a few simple ingredients, you can easily make this healthy and easy dinner for kids. Here's how to get it done:

1. Start off by preheating the oven to 190°C/375°F/gas 5. Peel the potatoes, then cut into thick chips. Parboil the chips in boiling salted water for 5-7 minutes, depending on how thick they are. Drain and leave to steam dry while you prepare the fish and batter.

2. Put the flour, baking powder and beer in a large bowl and whisk together until smooth. Dust the fish fillets with a little extra flour, then dip in the batter to coat.

3. Heat the oil in a deep-fat fryer or large saucepan until it reaches 180°C/350°F on a cooking thermometer. Carefully place the chips into the hot fat and fry for 10 minutes or until golden. Drain well on kitchen paper.

4. Reheat the oil until it reaches 190°C/375°F on a cooking thermometer, then deep-fry the fish in batches for 5 minutes or until cooked through and golden. Drain well on kitchen paper and season with salt while still hot.

5. Place the chips onto a baking tray, then cook for 15-20 minutes in the preheated oven until crisp. Serve with the fish and mushy peas, and garnish with fresh mint leaves if desired. Enjoy!

Fish and chips is a great dish to make at home, offering delicious flavors and a healthy dinner option for the whole family. With just a few ingredients, it's easy to whip up in no time. Enjoy!

Beef Tacos

Ingredients

1 lb lean ground beef
1 medium onion, chopped
1 teaspoon chili powder
1/2 teaspoon salt
1/2 teaspoon garlic powder
1 can (8 oz) tomato sauce
1 box (4.6 oz) Old El Paso™ Crunchy Taco Shells (12 Count)
1 1/2 cups shredded Cheddar cheese (6 oz)
2 cups shredded lettuce
2 medium tomatoes, chopped
3/4 cup Old El Paso™ Thick 'n Chunky salsa
3/4 cup sour cream, if desired

Beef tacos are a healthy and easy dinner for kids. With just a few simple ingredients, you can whip up a tasty taco meal in no time! To get started, brown the ground beef with the onion in a large skillet over medium heat. Once it's cooked through, add chili powder, salt and garlic powder to the ground beef. Stir in the tomato sauce and let it simmer for 5 minutes. To prepare the tacos, heat up a taco shell according to package instructions. Fill each taco shell with the beef mixture and top with cheese, lettuce, tomatoes and salsa. Finish off your tacos with a dollop of sour cream if desired! Serve this yummy treat for dinner tonight and watch how quickly your kids devour it. Bon appetit!

Fettuccine Alfredo

Ingredients

1 pound fettuccine noodles (use gluten-free, legume, or zucchini noodles if desired)
4 garlic cloves.
1 small head cauliflower (1 1/2 to 2 pounds), enough for 6 cups florets.
4 tablespoons olive oil.
1 cup raw unsalted cashews.
2 cups vegetable broth.
⅛ teaspoon onion powder.
1/8 + ¼ teaspoon ground black pepper.

ettuccine Alfredo is a healthy pasta dish that you can easily prepare in the comfort of your own home. To make this healthy version, start by boiling the fettuccine noodles according to package instructions. Meanwhile, mince the garlic cloves and cut the head of cauliflower into florets. Heat olive oil in a pan and add the garlic and cauliflower florets. Cook until the cauliflower is tender, stirring occasionally. In a high-speed blender, add the cashews, vegetable broth, onion powder, and black pepper and blend on high speed until smooth. Pour the sauce over the cooked fettuccine noodles and mix to combine. Serve warm and enjoy! With this healthy pasta dish, you can have a delicious meal that's sure to please. Bon Appetit!

White Pizza

White pizza is a delicious and unique alternative to the traditional red sauce-topped pizzas. This delicious, garlicky white pizza recipe is sure to be a hit! Prepared with the right ingredients, it can make for a delicious lunch or dinner dish.

To prepare this delicious white pizza, you will need: dough for one large pizza, two tablespoons of olive oil, three minced garlic cloves, eight ounces ball fresh mozzarella sliced thinly, 1/3 cup ricotta cheese, 1/2 teaspoon kosher salt, 1/4 teaspoon freshly ground black pepper, 1/8 teaspoon dried oregano, 1/8 teaspoon dried thyme and 1/3 cup freshly grated Pecorino Romano or Parmesan cheese.

Start by preheating your oven to 375°F and lightly greasing a large, rimmed baking sheet. Unroll the pizza dough onto the pan and press it out into an even thickness. Then, brush the olive oil over the surface of the dough and sprinkle with minced garlic cloves. Layer thinly-sliced mozzarella over top of the garlic and drizzle with ricotta cheese. Sprinkle with salt, pepper, oregano and thyme. Finally, top everything off with freshly grated Pecorino Romano or Parmesan cheese.

Place in preheated oven and bake for 15 to 20 minutes until the crust is golden brown and delicious! Serve hot and enjoy!

This delicious white pizza is sure to be a hit with the whole family. With its garlicky flavor and delicious cheese-topped crust, it makes for a delicious lunch or dinner dish. So why not give this delicious recipe a try tonight? You won't regret it!

Chicken Tortellini

Ingredients

2 tablespoons olive oil.
8 oz boneless skinless chicken breast, cut into 1/4-inch slices.
3 cups fresh small broccoli florets.
2 teaspoons chopped garlic.
1 1/2 cups Progresso™ chicken broth (from 32-oz carton)
2 packages (9 oz each) refrigerated cheese tortellini.
1 cup milk.

Preparing a healthy and easy dinner for the kids doesn't have to be a hassle. This delicious Chicken Tortellini is sure to please everyone at the table.

To make this dish, start by heating two tablespoons of olive oil in a large skillet over medium-high heat. Once it's hot, add the chicken slices and cook for about 4 minutes until they're no longer pink. Add the broccoli florets, garlic, and a pinch of salt, then cook for another 3 to 4 minutes.

Next, pour in the Progresso™ chicken broth and bring it to a boil over high heat. Once boiling, add the tortellini and cook for about 8 minutes until the pasta is cooked through. Then, reduce the heat to low and stir in the milk. Simmer for a few more minutes until it thickens up a bit. Taste and season with salt and pepper if needed.

Serve the tortellini with some extra grated Parmesan cheese on top. Enjoy! This Chicken Tortellini is a healthy and delicious dinner that your kids are sure to love. It's quick and easy, ready in just 30 minutes. Enjoy!

*Note: You can customize this dish with other vegetables like mushrooms, bell peppers or spinach. For added protein, you can also add shrimp or cooked sausage. Enjoy!

Enjoy! With its delicious flavor and simple preparation, this Chicken Tortellini is a surefire winner for any family dinner. It's the perfect healthy and easy dinner for kids - ready in just 30 minutes! Bon appetit!

Bolognese Spaghetti

Ingredients
1 tbsp olive oil.
4 rashers smoked streaky bacon, finely chopped.
2 medium onions, finely chopped.
2 carrots, trimmed and finely chopped.
2 celery sticks, finely chopped.
2 garlic cloves finely chopped.
2-3 sprigs rosemary leaves picked and finely chopped.
500g beef mince.

If you're looking for delicious recipes for kids, look no further than bolognese spaghetti! This classic Italian pasta dish is packed with flavour and can be made in no time. Plus, children of all ages will love it! Here's how to cook the perfect bolognese spaghetti:

Begin by heating 1 tablespoon of olive oil in a large frying pan. Add 4 finely chopped rashers of smoked streaky bacon, 2 finely chopped onions, 2 trimmed and finely chopped carrots, 2 finely chopped celery sticks, 2 finely chopped garlic cloves and the leaves from 2-3 sprigs of rosemary that have been picked and finely chopped. Cook the ingredients until the bacon and vegetables are softened.

Next, add 500g of beef mince to the pan and season with salt and pepper. Stir everything together and cook for about 10 minutes until the mince is browned. Finally, pour in a jar or can of tomato sauce or passata, along with a little water if necessary. Simmer for 10 minutes, then serve over cooked hot spaghetti.

Your delicious bolognese spaghetti dish is now ready to be enjoyed. Add a sprinkle of grated cheese and a dash of chilli flakes if desired. Bon appétit!

Coconut Yogurt Cake

Ingredients:

2 eggs
¾ cup (180ml) light-flavoured extra virgin olive oil
1 cup (280g) natural Greek-style (thick) yoghurt
2 tablespoons lemon juice
½ cup (110g) caster (superfine) sugar
½ cup (180g) honey
1 cup (80g) desiccated coconut
1¾ cups (225g) white spelt flour
1 teaspoon baking powder
½ teaspoon baking soda
½ teaspoon salt

Instructions:

Preheat the oven to 160°C/320°F.

Grease and line a 22cm round cake tin.

In a large mixing bowl, beat the eggs until light and fluffy.

Add the olive oil, yoghurt, lemon juice, caster sugar, and honey to the bowl, and whisk until well combined.

Fold in the desiccated coconut.

In a separate bowl, sift the spelt flour, baking powder, baking soda, and salt.

Gradually fold the flour mixture into the egg mixture until just combined.

Pour the mixture into the prepared cake tin and smooth the surface with a spatula.

Bake in the preheated oven for 50-60 minutes, or until a skewer inserted into the center of the cake comes out clean.

Remove the cake from the oven and allow it to cool in the tin for 10 minutes.

Turn the cake out onto a wire rack and allow it to cool completely.

Serve the coconut yoghurt cake with a dollop of Greek yoghurt and fresh berries on top.

Enjoy your delicious Coconut Yoghurt Cake!

Lemon Meringue Pie

Ingredients:

Homemade Pie Crust
5 large egg yolks (use the whites in the meringue below)
1 and 1/3 cups (320ml) water
1 cup (200g) granulated sugar
1/3 cup (38g) cornstarch
1/4 teaspoon salt
1/2 cup (120ml) fresh lemon juice
1 Tablespoon lemon zest

For the Meringue:

5 large egg whites
1/2 teaspoon cream of tartar
1/2 cup (100g) granulated sugar
1/2 teaspoon vanilla extract

Instructions:

Preheat the oven to 190°C/375°F.

Roll out the homemade pie crust and place it into a 9-inch pie dish. Crimp the edges.

Blind bake the pie crust by placing a sheet of parchment paper over the crust and filling the dish with pie weights or dry beans. Bake for 15 minutes, then remove the weights and parchment paper and bake for an additional 8-10 minutes, or until the crust is golden brown. Allow the crust to cool completely.

In a medium saucepan, whisk together the egg yolks and water.

Add the sugar, cornstarch, and salt to the saucepan and whisk until well combined.

Cook the mixture over medium heat, whisking constantly, until it thickens and comes to a boil.

Continue to whisk the mixture for 1-2 minutes until it becomes very thick.

Remove the saucepan from the heat and whisk in the lemon juice and lemon zest.

Pour the lemon filling into the cooled pie crust.

In a large mixing bowl, beat the egg whites and cream of tartar with an electric mixer until foamy.

Gradually add the sugar to the egg whites, beating until stiff peaks form.

Beat in the vanilla extract.

Spread the meringue over the lemon filling, being sure to spread it all the way to the edges of the crust.

Use the back of a spoon to create peaks in the meringue.

Bake the pie for 10-12 minutes, or until the meringue is golden brown.

Remove the pie from the oven and allow it to cool completely.

Chill the lemon meringue pie in the refrigerator for at least 2 hours before serving.

Enjoy your delicious Lemon Meringue Pie!

Greek Pasta Salad

Greek Pasta Salad is a vegetarian recipe that can be enjoyed by kids and adults alike. It's a healthy, vibrant dish with plenty of flavor to keep everyone happy! To make this delicious salad, start by boiling 12 ounces of mini farfalle pasta according to package instructions. Drain and set aside to cool. While the pasta is cooling, prepare the other ingredients: halve and pit 1/2 cup Kalamata olives; dice 1/3 cup red onion; cut 2 cups English or Persian cucumbers into half moons; halve 2 cups (1 pint) cherry tomatoes; dice 1 cup green bell pepper; chop 1/4 cup parsley; cube 1/2 cup feta cheese.

Once all the ingredients are ready, combine them in a large bowl. Add the cooled pasta, olives, red onion, cucumbers, tomatoes, bell pepper, parsley and feta cheese. Mix everything together until evenly combined. Serve chilled or at room temperature. Enjoy!

This vegetarian recipe is sure to be a hit with your kids. Not only is it healthy and full of flavor but it's also easy to make. You can prepare all the components ahead of time and let everyone customize their own bowl with their favorite ingredients. Greek Pasta Salad is perfect for lunchboxes or as part of a special weekend meal. Bon appétit!

Tagliatelle With Vegetable Ragu

Are you looking for delicious recipes that your kids will love? Look no further than tagliatelle with vegetable ragu! This delicious Italian-inspired dish is quick and easy to cook, making it perfect for busy parents. With just a few simple ingredients, you can create a delicious dinner in no time.

To make the delicious tagliatelle with vegetable ragu, you'll need: 1 onion, finely chopped; 2 celery sticks, finely chopped; 2 carrots, diced; 4 garlic cloves, crushed; 1 tbsp each of tomato purée and balsamic vinegar; 250g diced vegetables such as courgettes, peppers and mushrooms; 50g red lentil; 2 x 400g cans of chopped tomatoes with basil; 250g tagliatelle (or your favourite pasta); 2 tbsp shaved parmesan (optional).

To begin, heat some oil in a large pan on a medium-high heat and add the onion, celery, carrots and garlic. Stir occasionally until softened, about 5 minutes.

Add the tomato purée and balsamic vinegar, stirring until evenly combined. Cook for a further 5 minutes.

Next, add the diced vegetables and red lentil to the pan and cook for around 10 minutes or until softened. Finally, add the canned tomatoes with basil, reduce the heat to low and simmer for 15-20 minutes.

Once the sauce is cooked, cook the tagliatelle according to the packet instructions. Once both are ready, you can serve with some freshly shaved parmesan if desired. Bon appetit!

Enjoy delicious meals made by your own hands with this delicious tagliatelle with vegetable ragu recipe! It's quick and easy to make, so it's perfect for busy parents who want delicious recipes their kids will love. Give it a try today!

Happy cooking! :)

Pan Pizza

Making delicious pan pizza is easier than you think with the right ingredients. To make your own delicious pan pizza, start by combining 2 1/4 cups of all-purpose flour and 1 teaspoon of kosher salt in a large bowl. Sprinkle in 3/4 teaspoon of active dry yeast, then add 3/4 cup plus 3 tablespoons of lukewarm water and mix until the dough comes together. Knead the dough on a lightly floured surface for about 5 minutes until it is smooth and elastic. Transfer the dough to an oiled bowl, cover with plastic wrap, and let rise for at least one hour.

Meanwhile, prepare the toppings by mashing two cloves of garlic with one tablespoon olive oil until it forms a paste. Spread one tablespoon of olive oil over the bottom of a greased 10-inch skillet, then roll out the dough in the pan until it covers the base. Spread the garlic paste and tomato sauce over the dough, sprinkle with some dried oregano, and bake for 18 to 20 minutes at 400°F. Enjoy your delicious pizza hot from the oven!

Making delicious pan pizza does not have to be complicated - all you need is some simple ingredients and a few steps to get started. With just a little patience and practice, you can create delicious pizzas that will impress anyone! Try experimenting with different toppings or flavor combinations to make new delicious recipes each time. So what are you waiting for? Get making delicious pizza in no time!

Happy cooking!

Rice Chocolate Pudding

Ingredients
1/3 cup medium-grain rice.
1/4 cup cocoa powder.
3 1/4 cups skim milk.
1/4 cup caster sugar.
canned pears, to serve.

Here's the method to go along with the ingredients:

Rinse the rice and place it in a medium-sized saucepan with 1 1/2 cups of water. Bring to a boil, then reduce the heat to low and simmer for 15 minutes, or until the rice is cooked and the water has been absorbed.
Add the cocoa powder, milk and sugar to the saucepan and stir to combine. Place the pan over medium heat and cook for 10-15 minutes, stirring frequently, until the pudding thickens and the rice is very tender.
Divide the pudding between four serving dishes and chill in the fridge for at least 1 hour, or until set.
Serve the pudding with canned pears on top. Enjoy!

Strawberry and Rhubarb Cobbler

Ingredients

4 cups (567g) rhubarb, diced.
1 quart (567g) strawberries, washed and sliced, or thawed if frozen.
1 cup (198g) granulated sugar.
3 tablespoons (32g) quick-cooking tapioca or 3 tablespoons (21g) cornstarch

For the fruit filling:

Preheat the oven to 375°F (190°C).
In a large bowl, combine the diced rhubarb, sliced strawberries, granulated sugar, and tapioca or cornstarch. Mix well and let the mixture sit for about 15 minutes, stirring occasionally, until the fruit has released some of its juices and the sugar and tapioca have formed a syrup.

For the cobbler topping:

In a separate large bowl, whisk together the flour, sugar, baking powder, and salt. Add the cold butter and use a pastry blender or your fingers to cut it into the flour mixture until it resembles coarse crumbs.
Add the milk and stir until a soft dough forms. It's okay if it's a bit lumpy.

To assemble and bake:

Transfer the fruit filling to a 9x13-inch (23x33-cm) baking dish or a similar-sized dish. Dollop the cobbler dough on top of the fruit in spoonfuls, leaving some gaps so the fruit can peek through.
Bake for 40-50 minutes, or until the cobbler topping is golden brown and the fruit filling is bubbling and thickened.
Remove from the oven and let cool for a few minutes before serving. Top with whipped cream or ice cream, if desired. Enjoy your delicious Strawberry and Rhubarb Cobbler!

Tuna Pasta

Ingredients

2 tablespoons olive oil.
2 large cloves garlic minced.
1 (5 ounce) can tuna, drained I prefer tuna packed in oil.
1 teaspoon lemon juice.
1 tablespoon fresh parsley chopped.
Salt & pepper to taste.
4 ounces uncooked pasta (I used spaghetti)

Tuna pasta is a delicious and easy-to-make recipe for kids. It's perfect for busy weeknights when you don't have much time to cook. To make this delicious dish, start by heating the olive oil in a large skillet over medium heat. Add the garlic and sauté until fragrant, about 1 minute. Add the tuna and stir to combine. Then add the lemon juice and parsley, season with salt and pepper to taste, and cook for another minute or two. Finally, add the uncooked pasta to the skillet and mix everything together. Cook according to directions on the box until al dente. Serve hot and enjoy! Tuna pasta is a delicious and nutritious meal that your kids will love. Enjoy!

Sesame Chicken Meatballs

Ingredients

1 pound ground chicken.
½ cup breadcrumbs.
2 tablespoons soy sauce.
1 tablespoon Shaoxing wine (or mirin)
½ tablespoon sesame oil.
1 tablespoon ginger, freshly grated.
½ teaspoon garlic powder.
2 tablespoons green onions, finely chopped.

These chicken sesame meatballs are a healthy and easy dinner option that your kids will love. To prepare the meatballs, simply combine all of the ingredients in a large bowl and mix together until everything is well-incorporated. Once the mixture is ready, form it into small balls with your hands. Place them on a parchment paper-lined baking sheet, and bake at 350°F for about 20 minutes or until the meatballs are cooked through. Serve hot with a side of your favorite vegetables or salad. Enjoy!

This is an easy recipe that requires minimal preparation time, making it perfect for busy weeknights. Plus, you can use leftover meatballs as a quick and simple lunch the next day. So when you're looking for a healthy dinner option that your kids will love, give these chicken sesame meatballs a try!

Spinach Ravioli

Making healthy pasta dishes is not only delicious but can also be easy to prepare. Spinach Ravioli is one such healthy option that you can easily make at home with a few simple ingredients.

To begin, start by combining the flours -200 g 00 flour and 100 g semolina flour- in a bowl. Then add the eggs, the egg yolk, 1 tablespoon of extra-virgin olive oil, and ½ teaspoon of salt. Mix until a dough is formed. Knead for about 5 minutes or until the dough has become smooth and elastic.

Next you'll need to prepare your spinach filling. Blanch 80 g of fresh spinach leaves in boiling water for 2-3 minutes and then puree until smooth. Drain the spinach to remove all of the moisture, then blot it with a paper towel or cheesecloth to ensure that no water remains in the spinach. Add this to your dough mixture and knead for an additional 5 minutes.

Using a pasta roller, roll out your dough into thin sheets, then cut into ravioli squares. Place a teaspoon of spinach filling in the center of each square and top with another piece of dough, pinching the edges together to seal.

Bring a large pot of salted water to a boil and add your spinach ravioli. Cook for 4-5 minutes until al dente. Serve with your favorite sauce and enjoy!

With these simple ingredients and instructions, you can easily make healthy spinach ravioli at home. Enjoy this healthy pasta dish for dinner tonight!

Baked Potato Bar

Ingredients

5 pounds baked potatoes.
3-5 pounds pulled pork cooked.
2 cups sharp cheddar cheese shredded.
1/2 pound bacon cooked & crumbled.
1 cup sour cream.
1/2 cup chives chopped.
2 cups broccoli cooked.
1 bottle bbq sauce.

A baked potato bar is an easy and healthy dinner option for kids, and it's simple to prepare. Start by baking five pounds of potatoes according to the instructions on the package. While they're cooking, pre-cook three to five pounds of pulled pork as well as one-half pound of bacon. Once the potatoes are done, split them open and sprinkle two cups of shredded sharp cheddar cheese over the top. Then, add the cooked pulled pork, crumbled bacon, one cup of sour cream, half a cup of chopped chives and two cups of cooked broccoli. Finally, make sure to provide some BBQ sauce for everyone to enjoy. With minimal effort, you can create a delicious and nutritious baked potato bar that all the kids will love! Enjoy!

Chicken Tortellini

Ingredients

2 tablespoons olive oil.
8 oz boneless skinless chicken breast, cut into 1/4-inch slices.
3 cups fresh small broccoli florets.
2 teaspoons chopped garlic.
1 1/2 cups Progresso™ chicken broth (from 32-oz carton)
2 packages (9 oz each) refrigerated cheese tortellini.
1 cup milk.

Preparing a healthy and easy dinner for the kids doesn't have to be a hassle. This delicious Chicken Tortellini is sure to please everyone at the table.

To make this dish, start by heating two tablespoons of olive oil in a large skillet over medium-high heat. Once it's hot, add the chicken slices and cook for about 4 minutes until they're no longer pink. Add the broccoli florets, garlic, and a pinch of salt, then cook for another 3 to 4 minutes.

Next, pour in the Progresso™ chicken broth and bring it to a boil over high heat. Once boiling, add the tortellini and cook for about 8 minutes until the pasta is cooked through. Then, reduce the heat to low and stir in the milk. Simmer for a few more minutes until it thickens up a bit. Taste and season with salt and pepper if needed.

Serve the tortellini with some extra grated Parmesan cheese on top. Enjoy! This Chicken Tortellini is a healthy and delicious dinner that your kids are sure to love. It's quick and easy, ready in just 30 minutes. Enjoy!

*Note: You can customize this dish with other vegetables like mushrooms, bell peppers or spinach. For added protein, you can also add shrimp or cooked sausage. Enjoy!

Enjoy! With its delicious flavor and simple preparation, this Chicken Tortellini is a surefire winner for any family dinner. It's the perfect healthy and easy dinner for kids - ready in just 30 minutes! Bon appetit!

Chocolate Pudding

Sugar-free chocolate pudding is a healthy dessert option for those looking to enjoy sweet treats without compromising their health goals. With just five simple ingredients, this no-sugar dessert recipe can be easily prepared at home and enjoyed as a guilt-free treat.

To make this delicious sugar-free chocolate pudding, you will need heavy cream, unflavored gelatin powder, powdered erythritol, cocoa powder, sea salt and vanilla. Start by heating up the heavy cream in a saucepan until it is just under boiling point. Add the unflavored gelatin powder and let it simmer until it has dissolved. In a separate bowl, mix together the powdered erythritol and cocoa powder. Add this mixture to the heated cream, stirring until all of the ingredients are fully combined. Lastly, add a pinch of sea salt and some vanilla for flavor.

Let the mixture cool in the refrigerator for a few hours before serving your sugar-free chocolate pudding. Enjoy as is or top with fresh berries for an added burst of flavor. This delicious no-sugar dessert can be enjoyed any day of the week, so you can indulge without compromising your health goals!

Enjoy this easy and healthy sugar-free chocolate pudding recipe today!

Apple Nut Muffins

Ingredients:

2 cups all-purpose flour.
1/2 cup granulated sugar.
3 teaspoons baking powder.
1 1/2 teaspoon ground cinnamon, divided.
1/2 teaspoon salt.
2 eggs.
3/4 cup milk.
1 apple, peeled, cored, and finely chopped (about 1 cup)

These healthy snack muffins are a great way to get kids to enjoy healthy food. Not only are they easy to make, but they also have the added bonus of containing nutritious ingredients like apples, eggs and all-purpose flour.

To prepare these healthy snack muffins, start by preheating your oven to 375 degrees F. In a large bowl, whisk together the flour, sugar, baking powder, 1 teaspoon cinnamon and salt. In another bowl, beat together the eggs and milk until smooth. Then stir in the apple.

Next add the wet ingredients into the dry ingredients and mix until blended. Spoon the batter into greased or paper lined muffin cups filling them about two-thirds full. Sprinkle the remaining cinnamon over the top.

Bake for 18-20 minutes, or until a toothpick inserted into the center of the muffin comes out clean. Let cool before serving and enjoy! With these healthy snack muffins, your kids will love healthy food without even knowing it.

Happy snacking!

Pesto Quesadillas

If you're looking for vegetarian recipes for kids that are both healthy and delicious, try making these pesto quesadillas! Perfectly cheesy and packed with flavour, they'll become a family favourite in no time.

To make the pesto quesadillas, start by thinly slicing one roma tomato and gathering 3/4 cup of fresh baby spinach. Add 1/4 cup of vegan pesto to the vegetables; if desired, adjust this amount to suit your taste preferences. Next, add 1/2 cup of vegan mozzarella shreds (we recommend Follow Your Heart or Miyokos) as well as 1/4 cup of optional vegan feta crumbles. Place all of the ingredients onto two large tortillas (gluten-free if desired).

Once all of the ingredients are in place, carefully fold the tortillas over and press down to secure the ingredients. Preheat a skillet over medium heat and lightly grease with oil or vegan butter. Place the quesadilla onto the hot skillet and cook for 1-2 minutes on each side until golden brown. Finally, slice into wedges and serve warm!

Your vegetarian kids will love these delicious pesto quesadillas! Enjoy as a main dish, healthy lunchbox treat, or snack. Bon appetite!

Chicken Noodle Casserole

Ingredients
12 oz. wide egg noodles.
10.5-oz. cans cream of chicken soup.
1 c. whole milk.
1 c. shredded sharp cheddar cheese.
1 tsp. ground black pepper.
1/2 tsp. kosher salt.
3 c. cooked, shredded chicken (from 1 rotisserie chicken)
1/2. small yellow onion, finely chopped.

Making a chicken noodle casserole is an easy and healthy dinner option for kids. To begin, preheat your oven to 400 degrees Fahrenheit. In a large pot over medium heat, cook the egg noodles according to package directions. Drain the cooked noodles and set aside.

In a medium-sized bowl, combine the cream of chicken soup, milk, shredded cheese, ground black pepper and kosher salt. Stir until the ingredients are completely blended.

In a 9-by-13-inch baking dish, spread the cooked egg noodles. Top with the shredded chicken and onion pieces. Pour the cream of chicken mixture over the noodles and chicken, spreading evenly to ensure everything is coated.

Bake for 25 minutes until the cheese is melted and bubbly. Let cool for about 10 minutes before serving. Enjoy!

This chicken noodle casserole provides a comforting, delicious and healthy dinner option for kids. It's quick to prepare, full of flavor and sure to please everyone at the table.

Macadamia Pesto

INGREDIENTS

2 CUPS TIGHTLY PACKED FRESH BASIL LEAVES.
1/2 CUP PARMIGGIANO-REGGIANO CHEESE GRATED.
2 GARLIC CLOVES PEELED.
1/2 CUP EXTRA-VIRGIN OLIVE OIL.
1 TEASPOON FRESH-SQUEEZED LEMON JUICE.
1/3 CUP MACADAMIA NUTS TOASTED.
KOSHER SALT AND FRESHLY-GROUND PEPPER TO TASTE.

This healthy Macadamia Nut Pesto is the perfect addition to your favorite pasta dish. To prepare, simply place the basil leaves, Parmiggiano-Reggiano cheese, garlic cloves and macadamia nuts in a food processor. Pulse until all ingredients are combined but still chunky. Slowly add in olive oil and lemon juice and mix until the desired consistency is achieved. Add salt and pepper to taste, and serve over your favorite healthy pasta dish! Enjoy! For an added crunch, you can garnish with a few more toasted macadamia nuts. Bon Appetit!

Chocolate Avocado Mousse

Avocado and chocolate mousse is a delicious no sugar dessert recipe that is also healthy. To make this decadent treat, you will need two ripe avocados chopped, 200g of good quality dark eating chocolate (60-75% cocoa) broken into pieces, ½ cup of your preferred milk of choice such as cow's, almond or coconut milk, and two tablespoons of liquid honey or pure maple syrup (optional).

To prepare the mousse, first melt the chocolate in a heatproof bowl over simmering water or in a microwave. Once melted, set aside to cool slightly. In a food processor combine the avocados and stir with melted chocolate until combined and smooth. Add milk and sweetener of choice to the mixture and blend together until light and creamy.

Transfer the mousse into separate bowls or glasses, cover with cling film, and refrigerate for 1-2 hours. When ready to eat, enjoy - this delicious no sugar dessert recipe is guilt-free! Enjoy!

You can also serve the mousse with some fresh berries or grated dark chocolate for a touch of sweetness. No matter how you choose to enjoy your avocado and chocolate mousse, it definitely is a healthy dessert that will satisfy all taste buds! Enjoy!

Veggie Pizza

If you're looking to make delicious veggie pizza, here's a delicious recipe that will get the job done. Start by preheating your oven to 425°F and preparing your ingredients. You'll need store-bought or homemade pizza sauce, vegan mozzarella cheese (optional), sliced red and green bell peppers, onions (white or yellow), mushrooms of your choice, olives (sliced black are traditional but other varieties like kalamata or castelvetrano can be delicious!), dried oregano, and fresh basil.

Instructions for assembling your pizza: spread the pizza sauce over a prepared crust and top with the cheese and veggies. Sprinkle with oregano before baking for 15-20 minutes or until the cheese is melted and the crust is golden. Finally, garnish with fresh basil before slicing and serving. Enjoy!

Creating delicious veggie pizza doesn't have to be complicated or time-consuming. With this simple recipe, you can make a delicious meal in no time. Whether it's for lunch, dinner, or a snack, you can rest assured that your pizza will be delicious every time! Bon appetit!

Creamy Tomato Soup

Tomato Soup is a great lunch choice for kids because it's easy to make and packed with healthy ingredients. Plus, they will love the bright and vibrant colour! Here's what you'll need to make this delicious tomato soup recipe:

- 1-1.25kg/2lb 4oz-2lb 12oz ripe tomatoes

- 1 medium onion

- 1 small carrot

- 1 celery stick

- 2 tbsp olive oil

- 2 squirts of tomato purée (about 2 tsp)

- A good pinch of sugar

- 2 bay leaves

Once you've gathered all the ingredients, it's time to start cooking! Begin by heating the olive oil in a large saucepan and adding the diced onion, carrot, celery stick. Cook over medium heat for about 5 minutes until softened. Then add the tomatoes, purée, bay leaves and sugar. Cover with a lid and cook for 40 minutes. Once the soup is cooked, remove the bay leaves and blend until smooth with a blender.

Serve up this delicious tomato soup with some crusty bread or croutons on top and you have an easy, healthy lunch that your kids will love! Enjoy!

Creamy Salmon Pasta

Ingredients
2 salmon fillets.
1 tbsp olive oil, plus 1 tsp if roasting.
175g penne.
2 shallots or 1 small onion, finely chopped.
1 garlic clove, crushed.
100ml white wine.
200ml double cream or crème fraîche.
¼ lemon, zested and juiced.

Creamy salmon pasta is a delicious and easy recipe for kids. This delicious meal can be prepared in just a few simple steps.

To begin, preheat your oven to 200°c (gas mark 6) and brush the salmon fillets with 1 tbsp of olive oil. Place them in the oven to bake for 12-15 minutes until cooked through. Once the salmon is cooked, flake it into small pieces and set aside.

Bring a large pot of salted water to the boil and cook your penne according to packet instructions until al dente.

Meanwhile, heat 1 tsp of olive oil in a large skillet over medium-high heat. Add the shallots or onions and garlic to the skillet and sauté for a few minutes until softened. Add the white wine, cream or crème fraîche, lemon zest, lemon juice and flaked salmon pieces. Simmer gently over low heat for around 5-7 minutes until the sauce has thickened slightly.

To serve, drain the cooked penne and combine with the sauce. Divide into plates and enjoy your delicious creamy salmon pasta!

This delicious recipe is sure to be a hit with all the family - even picky eaters will love it! With only a few simple ingredients, this meal can be prepared in no time at all so why not give it a try tonight? Enjoy!

Strawberry Toast

Strawberry Toast is a healthy and tasty breakfast option for kids that's easy to prepare. To make it, start by melting the butter in a medium-sized skillet over medium heat. Add the sliced strawberries and cook for 5 minutes or until the berries have softened. Next, add the maple syrup, orange zest, non-fat milk, and teaspoon of salt. Cook for another 3 minutes or until the mixture thickens. Finally, place the slices of cinnamon raisin bread in a single layer on top of the strawberry mixture. Crack three eggs over the toast and let cook until the whites are set and yolks have just started to become soft. Serve immediately with a sprinkle of extra orange zest. Enjoy!

Cheesy Slaty Sticks

Ingredients

250 g (2 cups) flour + some for the rolling.
250 g (~1 cup) butter, room temperature.
250 g (1 1/4 cups) cottage cheese.
pinch of salt.
1 egg.
150 g (or more) (1 1/2 cups) Gouda cheese.

Cheesy Salty Sticks are healthy snacks that kids love. Preparing them is easy and straightforward; all you need are a few ingredients and some free time. To begin, combine 250g of flour with 250g of butter at room temperature in a bowl. Make sure the mixture is even throughout the bowl before adding a pinch of salt and 250g of cottage cheese. Once everything is properly mixed, knead the dough until it becomes firm and you can form a ball. Place the dough in the fridge for about an hour, this will make it easier to work with later on.

Once the dough has cooled down, stretch it onto a lightly floured surface and roll out the dough with a rolling pin. Use a knife to cut the rolled-out dough into strips, and then use a cheese grater to grate 150g of Gouda cheese over the strips. Once you have added the cheese all over, fold each strip in half and twist it gently. Place the twisted strips on a baking sheet lined with parchment paper and brush them with a beaten egg. Bake your Cheesy Salty Sticks in the oven at 180°C (350°F) for about 15 minutes until they are golden brown and crispy. Enjoy!

Pumpkin Pie

INGREDIENTS

1 (15-OUNCE) CAN PUMPKIN PUREE.
1 (12-OUNCE) CAN EVAPORATED MILK.
3 LARGE EGGS.
3/4 CUP GRANULATED ARTIFICIAL SWEETENER, SUCH AS SPLENDA OR TRUVIA.
1 TEASPOON GROUND CINNAMON.
1/2 TEASPOON GROUND GINGER.
1/4 TEASPOON GROUND NUTMEG.
1/4 TEASPOON SALT.

Pumpkin pie is a classic no sugar dessert recipe that can be enjoyed any time of the year. It's a healthy alternative to other high-sugar desserts, and it won't break the calorie bank. Preparing a pumpkin pie is easy with just a few simple steps.

First, preheat your oven to 350°F and grease a 9-inch pie pan.

In a large bowl, mix together 1 (15-ounce) can of pumpkin puree, 1 (12-ounce) can evaporated milk, 3 large eggs, 3/4 cup granulated artificial sweetener such as Splenda or Truvia, 1 teaspoon ground cinnamon, 1/2 teaspoon ground ginger, 1/4 teaspoon ground nutmeg, and 1/4 teaspoon salt. Whisk everything together until combined.

Pour the mixture into the prepared pie pan and bake for 50-55 minutes or until a knife inserted into the center of the pie comes out clean. Let cool before serving. Enjoy!

Vegetarian Chilli Mac

Ingredients

1 tablespoon olive oil.
1 cup chopped onion.
1 bell pepper (chopped small, any color)
2 medium carrots (chopped into ¼-inch pieces)
3 cloves garlic (minced)
1 tablespoon chili powder.
1 ½ teaspoons ground cumin.

Vegetarian chilli mac is an easy, healthy vegetarian recipe that can be enjoyed by kids of all ages. With simple ingredients like onions, bell peppers, carrots and garlic, this dish packs in plenty of flavor and nutrition. To prepare vegetarian chilli mac, start by heating the olive oil in a large pot over medium-high heat. Add the chopped onion and sauté for two minutes until softened. Then add the bell pepper, carrots and garlic to the pot and cook for three more minutes until vegetables are softened. Next, stir in chili powder, cumin and salt; reduce heat to low and simmer for five minutes more. Finally, serve vegetarian chilli mac with your favorite toppings such as shredded cheese or sour cream! This vegetarian recipe is a perfect way to get your kids to eat their veggies and enjoy the flavors of a delicious meal. With vegetarian chilli mac, you can rest assured that your family is eating healthy and enjoying every bite!

Chicken Noodle Soup

Ingredients
2 tablespoons unsalted butter.
1 onion, diced.
2 carrots, peeled and diced.
2 celery ribs, diced.
3 cloves garlic, minced.
8 cups chicken stock.
2 bay leaves.
Kosher salt freshly ground black pepper, to taste.

Chicken noodle soup is a delicious, healthy and easy dinner option for kids. To prepare it, start by melting the butter over medium heat in a large pot. Add the onion, carrots and celery to the pot and cook until softened, about 5 minutes. Stir in garlic until fragrant, about 1 minute. Pour in chicken stock, bay leaves, salt and pepper. Bring the soup to a boil. Reduce heat and simmer for 15 minutes or until the vegetables are tender. Finally, add noodles and cook according to package instructions. Serve hot with your favorite toppings such as shredded cheese, croutons or chopped parsley. Enjoy!

Ricotta Pasta

Ingredients

12 ounces bucatini or spaghetti.
1 cup ricotta cheese.
1 tablespoon olive oil.
½ cup grated Parmesan cheese, plus more to garnish.
½ teaspoon kosher salt.
Fresh ground black pepper.
Zest of 1 lemon (plus reserve some for garnish)
¼ cup pasta water.

This healthy pasta dish combines classic Italian flavors with the deliciousness of ricotta cheese. The result is a healthy but hearty meal that you can prepare in just 30 minutes. To make ricotta pasta, start by boiling 12 ounces of bucatini or spaghetti according to package directions and reserving ¼ cup of the cooking liquid before draining. In a large skillet, heat one tablespoon of olive oil over medium-high heat. Add the cooked pasta and ¾ cup ricotta cheese and stir until it's well combined. Sprinkle with ½ teaspoon kosher salt and a few grinds of black pepper. Add the grated Parmesan cheese, lemon zest and reserved cooking liquid to the skillet and stir to incorporate. Serve with extra Parmesan cheese and lemon zest for garnish. Enjoy this healthy pasta dish as a quick, easy weeknight meal or serve it as part of a special occasion dinner. Bon Appetit!

Cream Cheese And Egg Sandwich

Egg on Toast is an easy and healthy snack that kids of all ages will love. It's simple to prepare - just heat a skillet over medium heat, add butter, crack in the egg and cook for 3-4 minutes before flipping and cooking for 1-2 minutes more until the yolk is cooked through. Spread herby cream cheese on the toast and top with the cooked egg. Serve it up with an 8-ounce glass of milk as a healthy snack that your kids will love! With minimal effort, Egg on Toast is a perfect healthy treat for your little ones. Enjoy!

Banana Smothie

Banana smoothies are healthy snacks that kids will love. They are easy to prepare and you only need a few ingredients. All you need is 1 cup of sliced banana (frozen is best, about 1 large banana), ¼ cup Greek yogurt (plain or vanilla), ¼ cup milk (dairy, almond, oat milk, etc.), and ¼ teaspoon vanilla extract. To make the smoothie, simply blend all of the ingredients until it's creamy and smooth. You can also add honey if desired for a sweeter flavor. Enjoy this healthy treat as a snack in-between meals or after exercise! It's sure to be a hit with your little ones!

For a fun twist, try adding different healthy ingredients to the smoothie such as chia seeds, flaxseeds, unsweetened coconut flakes or even a handful of spinach. Whatever your kids enjoy will work great! Serve with some homemade granola for an extra special treat that's healthy and delicious.

The possibilities are endless when it comes to healthy snacks and banana smoothies are just one option. There are many other healthy snacks you can prepare for your family. Start exploring today and create healthy treats everyone in your family will enjoy!

Straciatella Gelato

Making a sugar free stracciatella gelato is easy, and it's a great way to enjoy a no-sugar dessert. To prepare this healthy treat, you will need 585 g of whole milk with 3.5% fat, 200 g of cream with 30% fat, 105g Perfecto-X, 15 g Perfecto-Binder-X, 95 g xylitol, a pinch of salt, and optionally 10g Stracciatella ICE PASTE Movito and 5g Perfecto-Cremosa.

Start by combining the whole milk, cream, Perfecto-X, Perfecto-Binder-X, xylitol, and salt in a pot. Heat the ingredients over medium heat while stirring until they reach a temperature of 82°C (180°F). Then, remove the mixture from the heat and pour it into a bowl before letting it cool at room temperature. Once cooled, cover the bowl with plastic wrap and place it in the refrigerator for 3-4 hours.

Once the mixture has cooled and set, churn it in an ice cream maker according to the manufacturer's instructions. When the gelato is nearly finished churning, add in the Stracciatella ICE PASTE Movito and Perfecto-Cremosa (if using). Churn until thick and creamy then scoop into a container and freeze for 2-3 hours. Your sugar free stracciatella gelato is now ready to enjoy!

This delicious no-sugar dessert makes a great treat any time of year. Try experimenting with different flavors by adding in fresh fruits or other ingredients to create your own unique recipes. With just the right amount of sweetness, you can enjoy a guilt-free treat that's sure to satisfy your sweet tooth. Enjoy!

This recipe for sugar free stracciatella gelato is sure to become one of your favorite healthy dessert recipes. Delicious, creamy, and satisfying - what more could you want? Try it out today and see how easy it is to make a no-sugar dessert that everyone can enjoy. Enjoy!

Green Smoothie

Tired of kids asking for unhealthy snacks? Want to give them something healthy and fun? Look no further than this delicious smoothie recipe! It's a great way to get in some leafy greens as well as healthy fruits, like mango, pineapple and banana. Plus it only takes minutes to prepare.

Start by tightly packing two cups of leafy greens into a measuring cup. Then, toss the greens into a blender with some water and blend until there are no more leafy chunks. Next, add in mango, pineapple and bananas for a healthy dose of nutrients. Blend everything together again until it becomes smooth.

Lastly, pour the delicious smoothie into a mason jar (or your favorite cup) and watch the kids enjoy healthy snacks. They'll be feeling like rawkstars!

Try this healthy smoothie recipe today, and make sure to get creative with your ingredients. Enjoy!

Vegan Mac And Cheese

Vegan mac and cheese is a vegetarian-friendly take on the classic dish that kids love. It's an easy, healthy recipe that can be quickly prepared any night of the week. To make vegan mac and cheese, you'll need 1 1/2 cups raw cashews, 2 cups water, 3 tablespoons fresh lemon juice, 1/2 cup nutritional yeast, 1/4 teaspoon turmeric, 1/2 teaspoon garlic powder and 1 1/2 teaspoons salt. For vegetarian recipes for kids, you can also add a 7-oz bag of shredded vegan cheddar cheese for extra flavor.

To prepare your vegan mac and cheese: first combine the cashews with the water in a blender or food processor until smooth. Next add the lemon juice, nutritional yeast, turmeric, garlic powder and salt. Blend until creamy and smooth.

Pour the mixture into a pot and cook over medium-high heat while stirring constantly. Once the sauce has thickened, remove it from heat and stir in the shredded cheese if using. Serve warm with your favorite vegetarian sides like steamed broccoli or edamame beans.

Vegan mac and cheese makes for a healthy recipe that kids will love as an alternative to traditional macaroni dishes. Enjoy!

Vegetarian Burger

Ingredients

1 x 400 g tin of chickpeas.
1 x 340 g tin of sweetcorn.
½ a bunch of fresh coriander , (15g)
½ teaspoon paprika.
½ teaspoon ground coriander.
½ teaspoon ground cumin.
1 lemon.
3 heaped tablespoons plain flour , plus extra for dusting.!

If you're looking for vegetarian recipes that are fun and healthy for kids, look no further than this vegetarian burger! This delicious vegetarian dish is easy to prepare and packed with flavour. With a combination of tinned chickpeas, sweetcorn, fresh herbs, spices and a squeeze of lemon juice, these vegetarian burgers are sure to please even the pickiest eaters.

To make the vegetarian burgers, start by draining and rinsing the chickpeas before placing them in a bowl. Add the sweetcorn and finely chopped coriander leaves. Mix together all of the spices - paprika, ground coriander, ground cumin - before adding them to the bowl along with a squeeze of lemon juice. Give it all a good mix before adding the plain flour to help bind it together.

Shape the vegetarian burger mixture into balls, then flatten them out into patties and lightly dust with flour before frying in a pan for around 3 minutes each side until golden brown and crisp. Serve your vegetarian burgers hot with your favourite accompaniments - from salad leaves to mashed potato! Enjoy!

Roasted Vegetables Pasta

This healthy roasted vegetable pasta dish is the perfect weeknight meal. The mix of vibrant vegetables and earthy flavors will keep your taste buds satisfied! For this recipe, you'll need 4 carrots, 2 Vidalia onions (or 1 small yellow onion), 5 small pattypan squash, 2 small zucchini, 10 cherry tomatoes, extra-virgin olive oil, sherry vinegar, and minced garlic.

To prepare the dish, preheat your oven to 425 degrees Fahrenheit. Place all of the vegetables on a large baking sheet and lightly drizzle with extra-virgin olive oil and season with salt and pepper. Roast for 25 minutes or until the veggies are soft and lightly browned.

In a large skillet, heat 1 tablespoon of olive oil over medium-high heat. Add the minced garlic and cook until fragrant (about 30 seconds). Add in the roasted vegetables, sherry vinegar, and cooked pasta. Toss to combine and season with salt and pepper to taste. Serve hot with an extra drizzle of olive oil. Enjoy!

Chocolate Cookie

Ingredients

2 cups white sugar.
1 ¼ cups margarine, softened. Great Value Margarine, 16 oz.
2 large eggs.
2 teaspoons vanilla extract.
2 cups all-purpose flour.
¾ cup unsweetened cocoa powder.
1 teaspoon baking soda.
⅛ teaspoon salt.

Instructions:

Preheat the oven to 350°F (180°C). Line a baking sheet with parchment paper.
In a large bowl, cream together the sugar and margarine until light and fluffy.
Beat in the eggs and vanilla extract until well combined.
In a separate bowl, whisk together the flour, cocoa powder, baking soda, and salt.
Gradually mix the dry ingredients into the wet ingredients until just combined.
Using a cookie scoop or spoon, form the dough into 1-inch balls and place them on the prepared baking sheet, leaving about 2 inches between each cookie.
Bake for 10-12 minutes, or until the edges are set and the centers are still slightly soft.
Remove from the oven and let cool on the baking sheet for 5 minutes, then transfer the cookies to a wire rack to cool completely.
Serve and enjoy!

Pesto Pizza

Are you looking for delicious pizza recipes? Making a pesto pizza is one of the best ways to enjoy a delicious and unique meal. With just a few simple ingredients, you can make this delicious homemade pizza in no time. Here's how to prepare it:

To start, preheat your oven to 425°F (220°C). Spread some cornmeal on your work surface and roll out the dough into desired size. Place the dough onto a baking sheet lined with parchment paper or lightly greased with olive oil.

Spread basil pesto over the dough using ½ cup of olive oil. Top with mozzarella cheese and roasted cherry tomatoes or sun-dried tomatoes. Bake in preheated oven until golden brown and bubbly, 18 to 20 minutes.

Once cooked, top with fresh basil and red pepper flakes for added flavor. Enjoy your delicious pesto pizza! It's a great addition to any meal or served as an appetizer. Bon appétit!

Black Bean Quinoa Tacos

Ingredients

2 tablespoons oil.
½ red onion diced.
1 jalapeño diced.
¾ cup quinoa dry.
1 15-ounce can black beans drained and rinsed.
2 tablespoons taco seasoning.
1 ½ cups broth or water.

If you're looking for vegetarian recipes for kids that are both healthy and delicious, look no further than this black bean quinoa taco recipe. This kid-approved vegetarian dish is simple to make and packed with flavor. Plus, it only takes about 30 minutes of prep time before it's ready to serve.

To start preparing this vegetarian recipe for kids, heat 2 tablespoons of oil in a large skillet over medium-high heat. Then add the diced onion and jalapeno and cook until tender, about 5 minutes. Once done, add the dry quinoa to the pan and stir until evenly coated with oil. Next, add the beans, taco seasoning and broth or water to the skillet and mix together. Bring to a low boil and reduce to a simmer, then cook until the quinoa is tender, about 15 minutes.

Once done, you're ready to assemble your black bean quinoa tacos. Serve with warm tortillas and your favorite taco toppings. Then enjoy this vegetarian meal that the entire family can love!

This vegetarian recipe for kids is sure to become a regular in your household, thanks to its delicious flavor and healthy ingredients. Plus, it only requires minimal prep time so you can easily prepare it on busy nights. Try out this vegetarian recipe for kids today and enjoy!

Vegan French Toast

Vegan French Toast is a vegetarian-friendly recipe perfect for kids. All you need is some sliced bread of choice, a banana (or coconut cream or flax eggs for a vegan version), nondairy milk, sweetener, and a pinch of salt. For added flavor, sprinkle on some optional nutritional yeast and cinnamon.

To prepare the vegan French toast, start by mashing the banana in a bowl until smooth. Alternatively, you can mix together coconut cream or flax eggs to achieve a similar consistency. Next, add the nondairy milk and sweetener, stirring together until combined. Finally, season with a pinch of salt and stir in optional nutritional yeast and cinnamon for extra flavor.

Once the French toast batter is ready, dip the slices of bread into the mixture and let it sit for a few minutes before cooking on a greased skillet over medium heat. Flip when golden brown and cook until both sides are evenly browned. Serve with your favorite toppings, such as vegan butter, syrup or fresh berries!

Brownies

1 EGG.
1 EGG YOLK.
1/2 CUP AVOCADO OIL.
1/2 CUP TRUVIA *
1 TSP VANILLA.
1/3 CUP ALL PURPOSE FLOUR 48G.
1/3 CUP COCOA POWDER 27G.
1/4 TSP SALT.

Making sugar free brownies is a great way to enjoy a healthy dessert without any added sugar. Here's how you can make some delicious and nutritious brownies in no time!

To begin, preheat your oven to 350 degrees Fahrenheit. Then, whisk together the egg, egg yolk and avocado oil until light and fluffy. Next, mix in the Truvia, vanilla, flour, cocoa powder and salt.

Once everything is mixed together, pour the batter into a greased 8x8 baking dish. Bake for 20 minutes or until a toothpick inserted in the center comes out clean. Allow to cool completely before cutting into squares. Enjoy with your favorite no sugar dessert recipes!

Making sugar free brownies is a great way to enjoy a sweet treat without the added guilt. The combination of high-quality cocoa powder and Truvia makes for an irresistible dessert that will satisfy your cravings without any added sugar. Plus, it's easy to prepare and can be enjoyed with other healthy dessert recipes! So next time you are in the mood for something sweet, try making sugar free brownies!

You won't regret it. Enjoy!

Cheese Crackers

Ingredients

6 ounces sharp yellow cheddar cheese, shredded (1 and 1/2 cups shredded)*
1 cup (125g) all-purpose flour (spoon & leveled)
1 and 1/2 teaspoons cornstarch*
1/4 teaspoon salt
6 Tablespoons (85g) unsalted butter, cold and cut into 6 pieces
2 Tablespoons cold water
optional: sea salt for sprinkling

Cheese crackers are healthy snacks that kids love. They are packed with protein, calcium, and healthy fats from the cheese and butter. Making them at home is easy too--all you need is a few simple ingredients!

To make your own cheese crackers start by combining the flour, cornstarch and salt in a medium bowl. Use a whisk to mix it all together. Then add your shredded cheese and stir until it's fully combined into the dry mixture. Now cut in the cold butter pieces using either a pastry cutter or fork until the mixture resembles coarse crumbs (it should look like wet sand when you're done). Finally add one tablespoon of cold water at a time while stirring with a wooden spoon until everything comes together in a ball.

Once your dough is ready, roll it out onto parchment paper or a lightly floured surface to about 1/8-inch thickness. Cut into desired shapes and place them on an ungreased baking sheet. Sprinkle with sea salt if desired and bake at 350°F (177°C) for 18-20 minutes or until golden brown. Enjoy these healthy cheese crackers as an afternoon snack!

I want to take a moment to express my heartfelt gratitude for your recent purchase of my recipe book. As a passionate food lover, nothing makes me happier than sharing my favorite recipes with others. Your decision to invest in my book not only supports my dream, but also shows your commitment to expanding your culinary horizons.

I sincerely hope that the recipes in the book will inspire you to try new things and add some excitement to your meals.

Thank you again for your support and for being a part of this journey with me. I hope my book will bring you many happy and delicious moments in the kitchen.

www.ingramcontent.com/pod-product-compliance
Lightning Source LLC
Chambersburg PA
CBHW041147110526
44590CB00027B/4152